POETRY BY CHARLES SIMIC

What the Grass Says

Somewhere Among Us a Stone Is Taking Notes

Dismantling the Silence

Return to a Place Lit by a Glass of Milk

Charon's Cosmology

Classic Ballroom Dances

Austerities

Selected Poems, 1963–1983

Unending Blues

The World Doesn't End: Prose Poems

The Book of Gods and Devils

Hotel Insomnia

A Wedding in Hell

Walking the Black Cat

Jackstraws

Night Picnic

The Voice at 3:00 a.m.: Selected Late and New Poems

Selected Poems, 1963–2003

My Noiseless Entourage

That Little Something

Master of Disguises

New and Selected Poems, 1962–2012

The Lunatic

Scribbled in the Dark

Come Closer and Listen

No Land in Sight

No Land in Sight

Poems

Charles Simic

Alfred A. Knopf, New York, 2022

THIS IS A BORZOI BOOK
PUBLISHED BY ALFRED A. KNOPF

www.aaknopf.com

Library of Congress Cataloging-in-Publication Data
Names: Simic, Charles, [date] author.
Title: No land in sight / Charles Simic.
Description: First edition. | New York : Alfred A. Knopf, 2022. |
"This is a Borzoi book"—Title page verso.
Identifiers: LCCN 2021040296 | ISBN 9780593534939 (hardcover) |
ISBN 9780593534946 (ebook)
Subjects: LCGFT: Poetry.
Classification: LCC PS3569.I4725 N62 2022 | DDC 811/.54—dc23
LC record available at https://lccn.loc.gov/2021040296

Jacket photograph: Ten Balloons, Albuquerque, New Mexico, USA.
1993. (image inverted) © Michael Kenna
Jacket design by John Gall

Manufactured in the United States of America
First Edition

FOR HELEN

CONTENTS

FOUR

O N E

FATE

Everyone's blind date.

ALL BUT INVISIBLE

Sickly fly, taking slow, painful steps
On a high and narrow parapet,
Past a long row of tall windows
With a view of the jagged skyline

And the sun setting beyond it
Indifferent to your plight,
Where to turn for help as the wind
Comes gusting off the Hudson River

Eager to sweep you off your feet
And make you crawl wingless
On some poorly lit street below
Along with others down on their luck.

DREAMING OR AWAKE?

A man runs after me in the street
Offering to sell me a pocket watch.
He looks like an old-time preacher,
Pale as a ghost and dressed in black.

The clock over the railroad station
Had stopped at five minutes to eleven.
The one over the savings bank
Swore it was almost three o'clock

When he accosted me with his watch
Whose lack of hands and numerals
He wanted me to study and admire
Before I gasped at his asking price.

I WATCHED THE WIND

Thumbing pages and pages
Of a thick encyclopedia
Thrown out with the trash,
In a hurry to find an answer.

WINTER MORNINGS

There used to be a row of movie houses
On this block of new buildings,
Where the homeless went to get warm,
Wives to forget their husbands,
And a boy or two to skip school,

Watching cowboys and vampires,
Bank robbers and chorus girls
Busy doing what they normally do,
Only to freeze on the screen
Staring baffled into the distance

Where fire engines and police cars
Could be heard wailing in the street,
And afterwards the sound of sleet,
Lashing at people hurrying to work
And leaving trails of wet footprints.

EVERYONE IS RUNNING LATE

One can see it by the way the birds
Dart back and forth, the squirrels
Race up a tree, the bits of trash
Scurry with each new gust of wind.

And yes! Here comes a young woman
In a dress too tight and heels too high,
Shouting and waving her arms to alert
The bus driver pulling from the curb,

While he eagerly steps on the gas
As if late for his own wedding,
His bride cooling her heels at city hall,
Eyeing strangers hurrying in and out.

THE MUSIC BOX

Ladies and gents hung in rows of portraits
In the living room of your town house,
Over a small cross and a music box
That nowadays plays only silence
To an audience of draped chairs and sofas,

Do you hear the homeless woman
Comfort a scared little dog by her side
As she spreads rags for their bed
Beneath the marble steps your servants
Used to scrub daily for dirty footprints?

MY POSSESSIONS

I have lots of dead friends
And streets I roam at all hours
With eyes open or shut,
Hoping to run into them.

I have many address books
With crossed-out names,
Two clocks and a dozen wristwatches
I haven't heard tick in years.

I have a large black umbrella
I am scared to open indoors,
As well as when I step outdoors,
No matter how hard it rains.

Like a cobbler lost in a shoe
He is repairing, I rarely look up
From what I am doing,
One foot in the grave, of course.

MY CITY

With its dimly lit streets
From black-and-white movies,
Trashy mystery novels,
And destitute people
Shivering in its doorways.

PARADISE LOUNGE

One sucker still left
In that dive across the street.
The woman sitting
In his lap topless,
Her smile frozen
Eyeing the one onstage
Stroking her crotch
And gasping for air
As if drowning in live mud.
The hell-like metropolis
Emptying at this hour.
Flies changing places
On a corpse, or so they say.

NOVEMBER

The crosses all men and women
Must carry through life
Even more visible
On this dark and rainy night.

ON THIS STREET

My mother carried me in her arms
Out of a burning building
And set me down on the sidewalk
Like a puppet bundled in rags,
Where now I stand years later
Talking to a homeless dog,
Half-hidden behind a parked car,
His eyes brimming with hope
As he inches forward ready for the worst.

WHERE DO MY GALLOWS STAND?

Outside the window
I looked out as a child
In an occupied city
Quiet as a graveyard.

DEAR LORD

Does the loud ticking
Of my alarm clock
Keep you awake?

Do you lie thinking
The stars in the sky
Were a big mistake?

THE MIRAGE

Like a cartoon of a man in a desert,
Fallen on his knees and dying of thirst,
Who suddenly sees ahead of him
A fresh pond and some palm trees,

Once on a train approaching Chicago,
I saw a snow-peak mountain
I knew perfectly well was not there,
And yet I kept looking, seeing even

A green meadow with sheep grazing,
When the clouds of black smoke
Swirling over the huge steel mills
Hid that lovely vision from my eyes.

PAWNSHOP WINDOW

A huge blonde doll
In short pink dress
Guarded by kitchen knives
Of every size
About to clap
Her chubby hands
As some Romeo tears
Himself from his date
And strides over
To admire the display.

OBJECT MATRIMONY

World-famous fire-eater
Seeking a tantric dancer
To join him on the sea bottom
And blow bubbles with him.

COULD THAT BE ME?

An alarm clock
With no hands
Ticking loudly
On the town dump.

T W O

THERE IS NOTHING QUIETER

Than the softly falling snow
Fretting over each flake
And making sure
It doesn't wake someone.

THE BIG LIE

The hush of a summer morning
Bathed in the light of the rising sun,
Moved me so much with its beauty
Never did I suspect a hoax,
Till I caught sight of a black cat
Crossing the yard in a hurry
And glancing over its shoulder
With mounting apprehension,
Before ditching my little paradise
That had given it the creeps.

FAMILY GRAVEYARD

Angry men and furious women
Buried side by side years ago,
Their curses and muffled sobs
Making trees shudder to this day.

THE MYSTERY

What do these mutts barking in unison
Up and down our road know
That we haven't learned yet?
Burglars breaking into a home.
A new bride hanging from a tree.

You'd think by now their owners
Would yell at them to shut up
And chase them all indoors,
Since they managed to wake
This whole damn neighborhood.

Unless it is something else tonight
That's got them all upset,
Like seeing a star call it quits
After millions of years
And take a long dive out of sight.

A HUGE OLD TREE

Fed up with its noisy leaves
And sweetly chirping birds,
Plus a young woodpecker
Drilling himself a new home.

ON YORK BEACH

These rough and surly waves
Look like they wouldn't mind
Drowning a pair of unhappy lovers
On this cold December evening.

ONE SUMMER

Someone played a flute
In the cemetery at night
While young girls danced
Naked among the tombstones.
Francis, the gravedigger,
Told us that and lots more,
So we went there one night
To see for ourselves,
But nobody showed up.
It got late and kind of spooky,
When we heard the flute
Wailing as if trying to coax
A big fat cobra to dance,
But we were too chicken
To go over and take a peek.

NEIGHBORHOOD DOGS

My wife went past them every day
Telling those who barked at her,
"Go home, little doggie, go home,"
Which puzzled them to no end,
Since that's where they all were
Fiercely guarding their homes
On a road nobody else walked,
But her and an old mutt who came
Along each day to keep her company
And who himself had nothing to say.

AN OLD WOMAN

Walking with dignified air
Down her driveway to the mailbox
Accompanied by a hen
Who stops as she does

To watch her mistress
As she pries open the lid
And takes a look inside
Before sticking her hand in

And finding no letter
Remains deep in thought
Before turning home
In the afternoon gloom

Alongside her companion
Who keeps nodding
And clucking to herself,
I told you so, you old fool.

THE POOR MAN'S HORSE

All skin and bones
And left in freezing rain,
His head hung low
As if saying a prayer.

SUNRISE

As if a witch or a holy martyr
Were being burnt at the stake.
Red snowflakes coming down
In the glow of the rising sun.
The shadow each tree clung to
Fleeing like a purse snatcher
As hot embers fall in my yard,
Inviting me to test my faith
By walking barefoot over them.

WHEN IN THE MOOD

The devil plays the harp
Like an angel in heaven,
And the slide trombone
Like a hot Dixieland band.

TWO WIDOWS

They say she'd wear a strapless black dress
And carry a martini glass in her hand
As she went to visit the cows at sundown
And tell them things she told no one else.

Or how she'd walk down to her pond, strip
And go for a swim with someone spying
On every move she makes as she wades in
Humming off-key a song from her youth.

Most likely, it was a neighbor, another widow,
Who'd been watching her all these years,
Sneaking up to her house almost every night,
Hoping to hear laughter and glasses clinking.

SNAPSHOT

He was caught
Sitting pretty
With a tough-guy
Look that said:

I've got it good,
And now you
Have it good, baby,
Whoever you are,

Seeing me fall
Into your arms
Out of a book
At a garage sale.

ADORABLE BED

Love of my life, I only wish
I could take you to Venice tonight,
Where you'd be my gondola
And I your singing gondolier.

WINDY DAY

Two pair of underwear,
One white and the other pink,
Flew up and down
On the laundry line,
Telling the whole world
They are madly in love.

CRICKETS

Blessed are those
For whom time
Doesn't run,
But drags its feet

Seemingly in no hurry,
Like that sailboat
Way out on the bay
Arrested in its flight,

Two gulls hurrying there
To see what's up?
And closer to home,
Crickets, crickets, crickets.

PYRAMIDS AND SPHINXES

For David Rivard

There's a famous street in Paris
Called Rue des Pyramides.
The Sunday I went to see for myself,
An old woman with a heavy limp,
Who could've been a hundred years old,
Overtook me in a great hurry,

Waving her cane and pointing
At something behind my back.
A guillotine chopping heads?
Some grand duke and duchess
Disembarrassed of their own
And raised for the crowd to cheer?

There was nothing of the kind,
Just a peeling poster on a café wall
With the Egyptian sphinx on it,
Blind and half-buried in the sand,
And still looking mighty pleased
To be advertising a famous aperitif.

THREE

LOOKING FOR TROUBLE

Didn't know I was doing it.
Had a notion I was living
A nice, quiet old age
Patting children on the head,
Feeding pigeons in the park.

My peace of mind ended
The night I found a man asleep
On my doorstep. *How can*
This be? I thought to myself
As I stepped over him carefully.

Three times I rose that night
And tiptoed to the door, trying to
Hear him breathe. At daybreak,
I took a cup of coffee to him,
But he was gone, leaving behind

His hat. Surely not far, I thought,
Walking out in my robe and slippers
Into the snow-covered street,
Peeking into doorways as I went,
Calling, "Hey mister! O brother!"

WEATHER FORECAST

Sunny day shadowed
By dark thoughts,
And come evening,
A sky full of clouds
In their tragic robes.

WALT WHITMAN

Sparrows and pigeons flock
To where he lies sprawled,
Long-haired and white-bearded,
His back against a wall
On this badly run-down block
Where the homeless come to die
And people stop to witness
This morning's miracle,
A young woman in high heels
Squatting on the sidewalk
While tearing up a loaf of bread
To feed the toothless old poet.

BIG SHOT

You, in a long black overcoat and hat,
Striding past me
On this busy downtown street
While giving me the air,
I have a hunch
You are the one who cracks the whip
Around here and gives
Two-bit grippers like me the gate.
Is that true, big shot?
Better hop into that long limo
Idling at the curb,
'Cause I'm getting hot under the collar
And may yet blow my fuse.

THE YOUNG LADY SAID

"I don't mind being cross-eyed,
So was Venus, I've been told,"
Said one woman to another
Leaving a crowded discotheque.

MEMORIES OF HELL

We were surprised by birds singing,
A little girl rocking a doll to sleep,
And a circus tent in a parking lot
With a troupe of performing dogs.

The stores, however, looked closed,
Except for a brightly lit tattoo parlor.
Persephone's children out in front
Chatting and laughing far into the night.

You want to know about the fires?
We saw flames rising everywhere
And buildings blackened by them
With windows the color of dried blood.

The lone beggar we bumped into
Wanted to tell us the story of his life,
But with Satan's palace still to visit
We made excuses and hurried away.

CIRCUS

There go the bear and the lion
In the night sky.
The troops of fire-eaters
And jugglers of burning torches
Are right behind them
Doing stunts not visible
To the naked eye,
But known to astronomers
And to our neighbor's dog
Notifying people in their beds
Tonight's show has begun.

ON THE WAY TO BINGHAMTON

Where you took a wrong exit,
Not realizing you'd done that,
As if asleep at the wheel,
Or driven by a premonition
Of something wonderful
Awaiting you in a pet shop
Where you stopped to ask for directions
And ran into a large parrot
Squawking about something
To the pretty saleslady
With large hoop earrings,
Busy feeding hamsters,
One of whom she called Dave.

MY DOUBLES

In my youth, women took me aside at parties
To tell me that I reminded them
Of a dead brother or a former lover
Who all wore round glasses like mine.
One of them lay in a tub with cut wrists,
Another went for a ride in a balloon
And hasn't been heard from ever since.
One played the piano so beautifully
Total strangers knocked on his door
Pleading to be allowed to come in and listen.
As for me, the last time someone saw me,
I was reading the Bible on the subway,
Shaking my head and chuckling to myself.

IN THIS HEAVY TRAFFIC

What if I were to ditch my car
And walk away without a glance back?
While drivers honk their horns
As I stroll into the nearby woods,

Determined, once and for all,
To swap this breed of raving lunatics
For a more benign kind who dwell
Long-haired and naked close to nature.

I'll let the sun in the sky be my guide
As I roam the countryside, stopping
To chat with a porcupine or a butterfly,
While subsisting on edible plants I find,

Glad to share my meal with a moose,
Or find a bear licking my face
As I wake from a nap wondering, *Where am I?*
Stuck in the traffic, you damn fool!

THE FUNERAL

The graveside tears and prayers over,
A dog came to bark as we walked
Between headstones, sneaking peeks
At the widow's skirt teased by the wind,
While an undertaker raced after us
Waving an umbrella someone left behind.

Meanwhile, we thought of our old pal
Looking pissed in his posh new coffin
As his wife's limo idled at the gate,
But where had she vanished just now?
Most likely behind some bush to pee
With a long ride home ahead of her.

LEFT OUT OF THE BIBLE

What Adam said to Eve
As they lay in the dark:
Honey, go and take a look.
What's making that dog bark?

I'VE BEEN THINKING OF

Madmen who wander night and day
The great cities of the world
Hearing voices in their heads
And stopping to quarrel with them.

IN THE AMUSEMENT PARK

Blood-curdling screams
Riding up and down
On the Ferris wheel,

Faces like a pack of cards
Tossed in the air by a gambler
Who just lost his pants.

And on the drive home,
Dark roadside bushes
With necking couples

Surprised by our headlights,
And ducking like ducks
In the shooting gallery.

TANGO

Slinky black dress
On a wire hanger
In an empty closet
Its doors slid open

To catch the draft
From an open window
And make it dance
As in a deep trance

The empty hangers
Clicking in unison
Like knitting needles
Or disapproving tongues.

THE INSOMNIAC

Stuffing angels and demons
Like sticks of dynamite
Inside his graying head
As he sits in his motel bed,

His tongue a lit fuse
With a dancing little flame
Setting his brain on fire
While whispering in his ear:

Seeing you gloomy like this,
On a swell June night,
You are either a village idiot
Or a god of some cursed tribe.

HOOT, LITTLE OWL

Are you there?
Is there a *there*
Truly out there?

Hoot or keep quiet,
Whatever you like.
The night is dark,

Even though later
There may be stars
Astounded to see us here.

FIRST THING IN THE MORNING

You eavesdrop on birds
Gossiping in your yard,
Eager to find out what
They are saying about you.

FOUR

SOME FOLKS OUT LATE

Unknown bird, you shrieked
Once, then twice more,
As if a knife neared your throat
In one of the huge trees
At the far end of the lawn.

It made the babe in his mother's arms
Stir restlessly in his sleep.
Earlier there'd been talk of war
And of the fine weather we are having,
When the night fell suddenly

Blurring our faces on the porch
With what remained unspoken
In the thickening darkness,
A lake of blood still visible,
Where the sun had just gone down.

THE CROW

Early this morning
Its blood-soaked wings
Rose high above me
Like huge scissors
Snipping at strings
Holding my puppet head
So it doesn't fall off
As my feet go jitterbugging
On the ice in the yard.

COME SPRING

Don't let that birdie in a tree
Fool you with its pretty song,
The wicked are back from hell
Doing all the vicious things
That had them sent down below.

They brought Satan along
To lend them a helping hand
As they think up new evils,
For his guile has no equal
Nor does his bottomless hate.

CASSIOPEIA

Great empires going to hell,
Their cities torn by crimes,
Must mean nothing to you,
Nor does this peaceful lake
Where you come to bathe.

Perhaps hearing us whisper
Your pretty name in the dark
As we hug each other tightly
Is as close as you ever get
To partake of love and its mysteries?

JUST SO YOU KNOW

None of these money-grabbing bastards
And their bored wives, thin as wasps,
Have a soul to sell, Mr. Devil.
You'd have better luck with their poodles,
Though some are quick-tempered
And may snap at your ankles.
However, if you still want to give it a try,
This old couple live in a penthouse
With a view of the Statue of Liberty.

I NEVER FORGET ANYTHING

That's my trouble!
Like that shoe box of ripped photographs
I came across on the town dump,
And helped myself to one
Of a couple in bathing suits
Holding hands on some tropical beach,
Whose heads and faces
The wind had swept away
While I busied myself
Studying what was left
Of their youth and of their beauty.

NIGHT THOUGHTS

Light frightens them. Darkness too.
They crawl into our beds,
Not to talk, but to whisper
The way one does in the morgue.

CELEBRITY SIGHTINGS

Tragedy and Comedy
Stepping out of a white limo
In oversized wigs
And diminutive skirts,
Blowing kisses left and right.

Bedlam of adoring fans,
Shoving and pleading
For one more glimpse,
When all of a sudden
Panic and screams ahead.

Is someone, we wonder,
Already lying stabbed
On the slick dance floor,
Croaking out a name
We are dying to hear?

The towering bodyguards
With shaved heads
And mirror-tinted glasses
Won't say or even deign
To acknowledge our presence.

IN THE LOCKDOWN

I might have gone stir-crazy,
If not for my memories,
Those lifelong companions
Cooped up with me for months
And eager to console me

With stories of men and women
Who withdraw from the world,
And endured years of solitude
And dark nights of the soul
Thriving in some hole-in-the-wall

Where they found lasting peace
Obeying a voice in their heads
Telling them to just sit quietly,
So that the quiet can teach them
Everything they ought to know.

RAINY EVENING

Someone catching sight
Of his reflection in a store window
Impersonating a person
With blood and guts
Fleeing from someone,
Yet afraid to look back
At the one in hot pursuit
With no more substance
Than a ghost picture
On black-and-white TV
In his dead parent's bedroom,
With its station off the air.

EL MAGNIFICO

These trees have been put under a spell
By some master of the art
Who pointed a finger at them
And ordered them to be still
As they've done so ever since,
Spooking the birds not to tweet,
The million leaves not to fidget
One long and hot summer day
Till he dons his black cape
And top hat and makes his exit
Under the cover of darkness.

SUMMER DUSK

You've been the love of my life,
Light lingering in the sky
At the close of a long day
Over the roofs of some city
Like New York or Rome,
As streets empty in the heat,
And shadows lengthen
And darken every room,
Occupied or still vacant,
Where some turn on the lamp
And others step to a window
To savor this fleeting moment
When everything stops
As if stunned by its own beauty.

MY LOVE

We are like a couple of frogs
Basking in a soup pot
Slowly heated on the stove,
Loving the lukewarm water

And calling on all frogs
In every pond and puddle
To hurry up and join us
In this tropical paradise.

They won't be able to resist,
Seeing family and friends
Splashing each other below
Without a care in the world.

DARK WINDOW

Of a crying woman
With her tears briefly lit
By the bright headlights
Of a slow passing car.

HOT SUMMER NIGHT

The lazy light of distant stars
And down here on Earth
The cheerful sound of a brook
Cooling a fat watermelon.

ALL OVER THE WORLD NOW

Lovers are undressing lovers
And cursing the buttons,
Big and small, and zippers
Stubbornly stuck half-open.

MY LIFE IS AS REAL AS YOURS

Said the cricket
In the thicket
As the summer ended
And night fell.

ON GROVE STREET

Night, dark goddess,

I saw you fleeing
As the day broke,

Like someone's secret lover
Sneaking out of their bed

And glancing back once
Hearing my footsteps.

THE WIND HAS DIED

My little boat,
Take care.

There is no
Land in sight.

ACKNOWLEDGMENTS

These poems were published in the following liter-
ary magazines, to whose editors grateful acknowl-
edgment is made: *The New Yorker, The Threepenny
Review, The Southern Review, Salmagundi, Iterant,* and
The Little Magazine.

A NOTE ABOUT THE AUTHOR

Charles Simic is a poet, essayist, and translator who was born in Yugoslavia in 1938 and immigrated to the United States in 1954. Since 1967, he has published more than twenty books of his own poetry, in addition to a memoir and numerous books of translations, for which he has received many literary awards, including the Pulitzer Prize, the Zbigniew Herbert International Literary Award, the Griffin Poetry Prize, a MacArthur Fellowship, and the Wallace Stevens Award. Simic was a frequent contributor to *The New York Review of Books* and in 2007 was chosen as poet laureate of the United States. He is an emeritus professor at the University of New Hampshire, where he has taught since 1973, and was formerly a distinguished visiting writer at New York University.

A NOTE ON THE TYPE

This book was set in Monotype Dante, a typeface designed by Giovanni Mardersteig (1892–1977). Modeled on the Aldine type used for Pietro Cardinal Bembo's treatise *De Aetna* in 1495, Dante is a modern interpretation of the venerable face.

Composed by North Market Street Graphics,
Lancaster, Pennsylvania

Printed and bound by Berryville Graphics,
Berryville, Virginia

Designed by Betty Lew